FLASHBACK HISTORY

VIKINGS

Dereen Taylor

PowerKiDS
press

New York

Published in 2010 by The Rosen Publishing Group Inc.
29 East 21st Street, New York, NY 10010

First Edition

Library of Congress Cataloging-in-Publication Data

Taylor, Dereen.
  Vikings / Dereen Taylor.
     p. cm. — (Flashback history)
  Includes index.
  ISBN 978-1-4358-5501-4 (library binding)
  ISBN 978-1-4358-5502-1 (paperback)
  ISBN 978-1-4358-5503-8 (6-pack)
  1. Vikings—Juvenile literature. I. Title.
  DL66.T39 2010
  948'.022—dc22

6 30 3

2009002624

Picture Acknowledgements: Cover front: Michael Holford; WF/Statens
Historiska Museum, Stockholm; Aalborg Historiske Museum: 13(t); Courtesy, Canadian Parks Service: p38;
Martyn F. Chillmaid: p14, p15(b), p16; C.M. Dixon: p17(r), p20, p26(b), p28, p31, p40; Forhistorisk
Museum, Moesgard: p19; Werner Forman Archive: p7, p9, p17(1), p30; WF/National Museum, Copenhagen:
p33(t), p34(b), WF/Statens Historiska Museum, Stockholm: p26(t), p32; WF/Stofnun Arnamagnussonar,
Iceland:p33(b); WF/Viking Ships Museum, Bygdy, Oslo: p36-37; Robert Harding Picture Library: p8(t),
p14, p29(1); Michael Holford: endpapers, p12-13, p22(b), p25(b), p29(r), p37(b), p39(b), p40(1), p41, p42;
National Museum of Ireland, Dublin: p22(t); Skyggna Myndverk: p18(b); Statens Historiska Museum: p15(t);
Stofnun Arnamagnussonar, Iceland: p12(t), p31(t); Universitetets Oldsaksamling, Oslo: p34-35, p37(t); David
Williams: p18(t), p39(t); York Archaeological Trust Picture Library, p8(b), p21, p23, p24, p25(t), p35(b),
p40(r).

Every effort has been made to clear copyright. Should there be any inadvertent omission, please apply to
the publisher for rectification.

Endpapers: This Viking carving was excavated from St. Paul's Churchyard, London, U.K. It shows a
battle between a lion and a serpent, and dates from around 1030 CE. It stands 18 inches high and was
set up by two Vikings named Ginna and Toki.

Manufactured in China

CONTENTS

Words that appear in **bold** can be found in the glossary on page 44.

WHO WERE THE VIKINGS?

Look at the two maps on page 9. The small map shows the countries the Vikings came from. The large map shows the places they went to between 780 and 1100 CE. This period is called the Viking Age. The Vikings were fierce fighters who raided towns and **monasteries**. The Vikings were also great adventurers. They traveled looking for new lands where they could settle down and farm.

▶ THE VIKING HOMELANDS

By the end of the eighth century, the Vikings wanted to leave Scandinavia to find new land to farm. As this photograph of Norway shows, there are lots of mountains in Norway. This made it difficult to find good farmland.

▼ METAL WORKERS

The Vikings melted the ore and made metal. Then they made the metal into cooking pans, hammerheads, and axes. Skilled metal workers made swords like the one below.

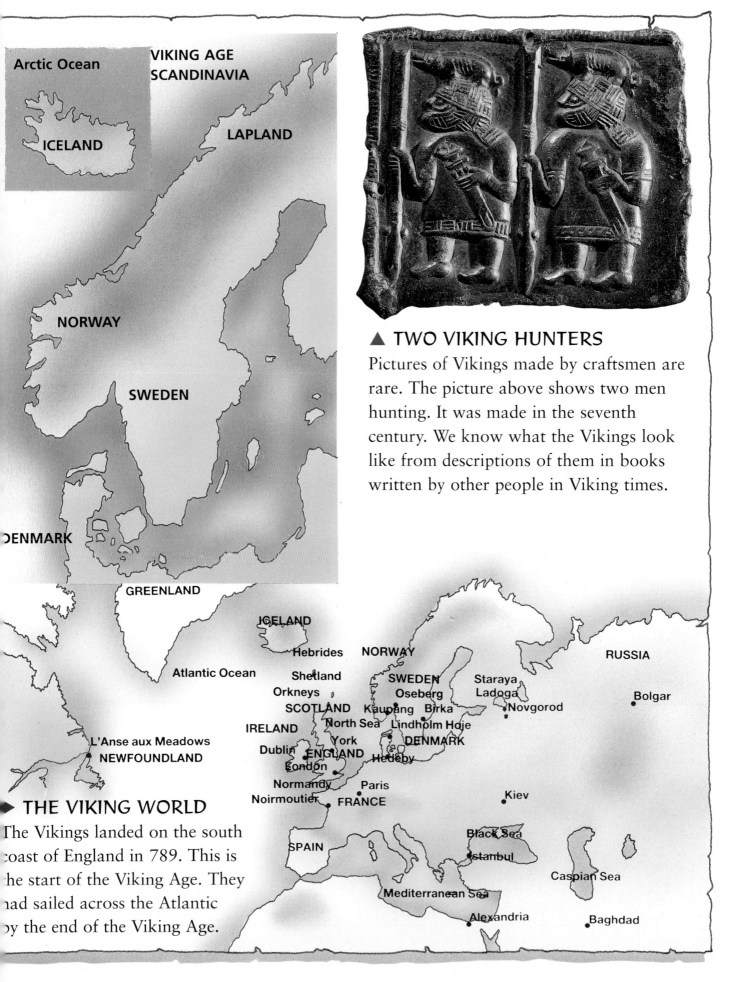

ICELAND

Arctic Ocean

VIKING AGE SCANDINAVIA

LAPLAND

NORWAY

SWEDEN

DENMARK

▲ TWO VIKING HUNTERS

Pictures of Vikings made by craftsmen are rare. The picture above shows two men hunting. It was made in the seventh century. We know what the Vikings look like from descriptions of them in books written by other people in Viking times.

GREENLAND

ICELAND

Hebrides

NORWAY

RUSSIA

Atlantic Ocean

Shetland

SWEDEN

Staraya Ladoga

Orkneys

Oseberg

Birka

Novgorod

Bolgar

SCOTLAND **Kaupang**

North Sea **Lindholm Hoje**

IRELAND

York

DENMARK

L'Anse aux Meadows

Dublin **ENGLAND** **Hedeby**

NEWFOUNDLAND

London

Normandy **Paris**

Kiev

Noirmoutier **FRANCE**

► THE VIKING WORLD

The Vikings landed on the south coast of England in 789. This is the start of the Viking Age. They had sailed across the Atlantic by the end of the Viking Age.

SPAIN

Black Sea

Istanbul

Caspian Sea

Mediterranean Sea

Alexandria

Baghdad

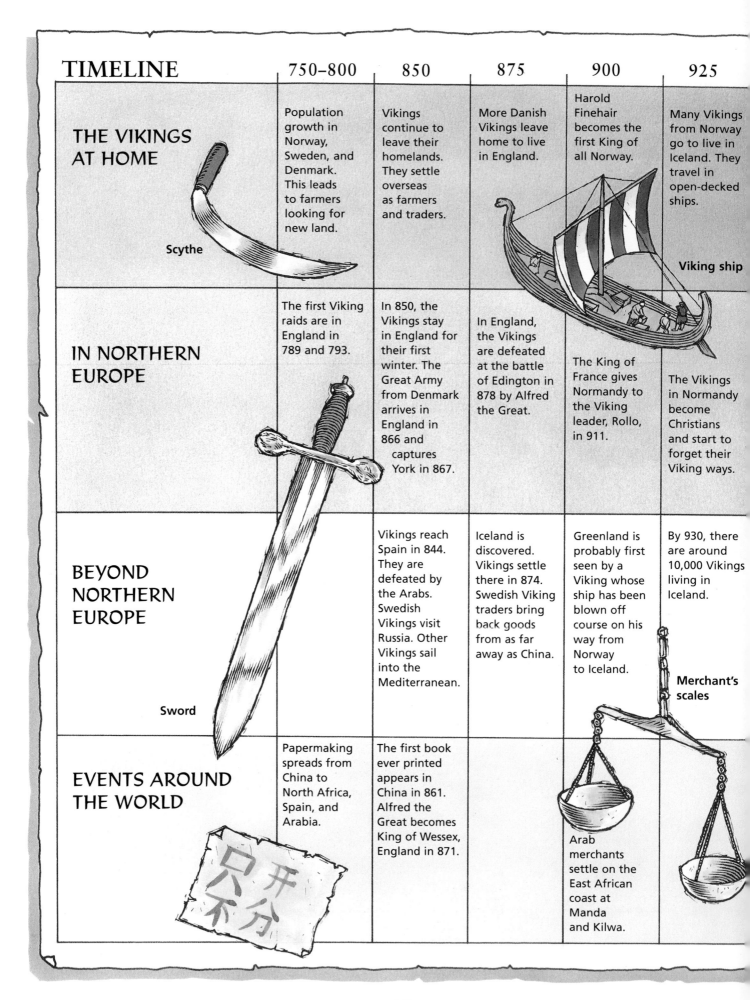

TIMELINE	750–800	850	875	900	925
THE VIKINGS AT HOME	Population growth in Norway, Sweden, and Denmark. This leads to farmers looking for new land.	Vikings continue to leave their homelands. They settle overseas as farmers and traders.	More Danish Vikings leave home to live in England.	Harold Finehair becomes the first King of all Norway.	Many Vikings from Norway go to live in Iceland. They travel in open-decked ships.
IN NORTHERN EUROPE	The first Viking raids are in England in 789 and 793.	In 850, the Vikings stay in England for their first winter. The Great Army from Denmark arrives in England in 866 and captures York in 867.	In England, the Vikings are defeated at the battle of Edington in 878 by Alfred the Great.	The King of France gives Normandy to the Viking leader, Rollo, in 911.	The Vikings in Normandy become Christians and start to forget their Viking ways.
BEYOND NORTHERN EUROPE		Vikings reach Spain in 844. They are defeated by the Arabs. Swedish Vikings visit Russia. Other Vikings sail into the Mediterranean.	Iceland is discovered. Vikings settle there in 874. Swedish Viking traders bring back goods from as far away as China.	Greenland is probably first seen by a Viking whose ship has been blown off course on his way from Norway to Iceland.	By 930, there are around 10,000 Vikings living in Iceland.
EVENTS AROUND THE WORLD	Papermaking spreads from China to North Africa, Spain, and Arabia.	The first book ever printed appears in China in 861. Alfred the Great becomes King of Wessex, England in 871.		Arab merchants settle on the East African coast at Manda and Kilwa.	

Scythe

Viking ship

Sword

Merchant's scales

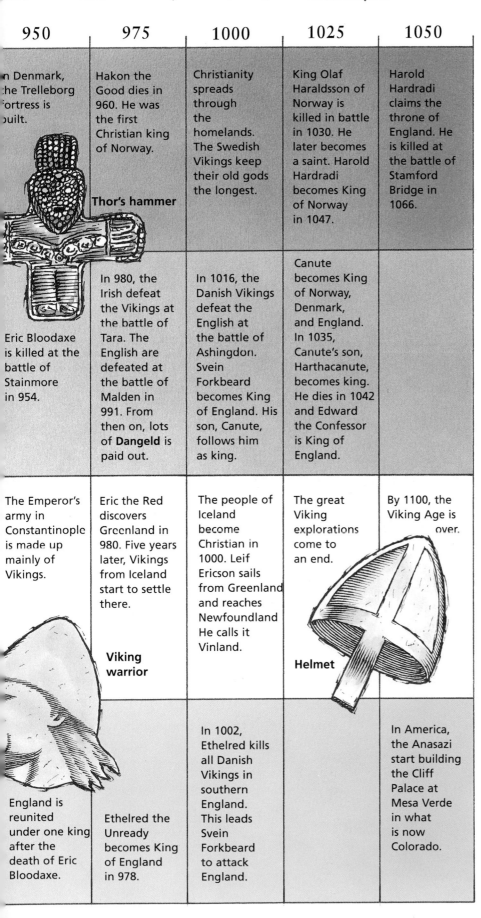

950	975	1000	1025	1050
n Denmark, he Trelleborg ortress is uilt.	Hakon the Good dies in 960. He was the first Christian king of Norway. **Thor's hammer**	Christianity spreads through the homelands. The Swedish Vikings keep their old gods the longest.	King Olaf Haraldsson of Norway is killed in battle in 1030. He later becomes a saint. Harold Hardradi becomes King of Norway in 1047.	Harold Hardradi claims the throne of England. He is killed at the battle of Stamford Bridge in 1066.
Eric Bloodaxe is killed at the battle of Stainmore in 954.	In 980, the Irish defeat the Vikings at the battle of Tara. The English are defeated at the battle of Malden in 991. From then on, lots of **Dangeld** is paid out.	In 1016, the Danish Vikings defeat the English at the battle of Ashingdon. Svein Forkbeard becomes King of England. His son, Canute, follows him as king.	Canute becomes King of Norway, Denmark, and England. In 1035, Canute's son, Harthacanute, becomes king. He dies in 1042 and Edward the Confessor is King of England.	
The Emperor's army in Constantinople is made up mainly of Vikings.	Eric the Red discovers Greenland in 980. Five years later, Vikings from Iceland start to settle there. **Viking warrior**	The people of Iceland become Christian in 1000. Leif Ericson sails from Greenland and reaches Newfoundland He calls it Vinland.	The great Viking explorations come to an end. **Helmet**	By 1100, the Viking Age is over.
England is reunited under one king after the death of Eric Bloodaxe.	Ethelred the Unready becomes King of England in 978.	In 1002, Ethelred kills all Danish Vikings in southern England. This leads Svein Forkbeard to attack England.		In America, the Anasazi start building the Cliff Palace at Mesa Verde in what is now Colorado.

THE AGE OF MIGRATIONS

The Viking Age came near the end of the Age of Migrations. This was a long period of time when many people were on the move across Europe. It started around the fifth century CE. Sailors crossed the North Sea and attacked Britain. At the same time, the Roman Empire was collapsing. Roman soldiers left Britain to defend Rome. When they had gone, **Angles, Jutes, Frisians,** and **Anglo-Saxons** moved to England. At the end of the eighth century, the Vikings left their homelands. They were looking for treasure, land, and trade in these new kingdoms.

THE LAST VIKING KINGS

In 1066, Harold Hardradi became King of England. He was killed at the Battle of Stamford Bridge.

DID THE VIKINGS GROW THEIR OWN FOOD?

Most Vikings were farmers who grew their own food. They usually had small farms and grew just enough food to feed their own families. In their fields, they grew grain crops including oats, barley, wheat, and rye. They also grew vegetables such as cabbages, onions, and beans. They kept geese and goats, as well as sheep, cattle, pigs, and hens.

▲ FISHING

Almost all Viking farms were near the sea. Most Vikings went fishing to catch cod or herring. They used a net or a hook on a line. Some fishermen speared fish from a boat. The fishermen in the picture above have caught a whale.

▼ FARMING

The picture below is from the Bayeux Tapestry. The tapestry was made at the end of the Viking Age. It shows how the Vikings farmed. First the land was plowed, then the seeds were scattered by hand. A horse-drawn **harrow** then covered the seeds with soil.

► A PLOWED FIELD

A lot of the Viking farmland is still farmed today. This means that the signs of Viking farming have gone. But some farms were not used after the Viking Age. In the center of this photograph, you can see part of a plowed field from Viking times.

► MAKING FLOUR

The Vikings made flour using two stones. One stone was twisted on top of the other, until the grain between the stones had been ground into flour.

▼ FARM TOOLS

Viking farmers used horses to pull plows and harrows. All the other work was done by hand. They used long-handled scythes to cut hay and sickles to cut grain crops. Hoes were used for weeding and spades for digging.

Trowel

Leaf knife

Scythe

THE VIKING SUMMER

Spring was a busy time on the farm. Fields were plowed and seeds were sown in the ground. Manure was spread on the hayfields to make the grass grow.

The farmer then probably went raiding or trading for the summer. His family would look after the farm. The farmer came back for the harvest at the end of the summer.

DID THE VIKINGS GO SHOPPING?

Most Vikings lived in small settlements with no stores. They made most of the things they needed, including clothes, tools, and furniture. But some towns

became **trading centers**. The main ones were Hedeby in Denmark, Birka in Sweden, Kaupang in Norway, and Jorvik (York) in England. In these towns, the Vikings could buy silk, glassware, and wine.

▼ POTS AND PLATES

This photograph shows **reconstructions** of Viking pottery, wooden plates, and bowls. The reconstructions are based on pieces found by **archaeologists** in York, in a street named Coppergate.

This name probably comes from two Viking words—*Koppr*, which means cup and *gat*, which means street. Most Viking cups and plates were made from wood. Clay cups and plates were more unusual.

HACK SILVER

Sometimes the early Vikings exchanged their goods for silver finger-rings and arm-rings. When they needed money, they cut pieces of silver off the rings. The silver was weighed on scales and used as money.

THE SHOPS AT JORVIK

This picture shows a Viking workshop, which has been rebuilt at the Jorvik Museum in York. This shop belonged to a leather worker. He made shoes, belts, and harnesses for horses.

Wooden spoon

MAKING A COIN

Coins were handmade by a moneyer. He engraved one side of the coin backward on a metal die (1). Then he put the **die** on a strip of silver (2) and tapped it with a hammer to make an imprint. He made a row of imprints on one side of the strip (3). Then he split the coins (4). He stamped the other side of the coin with a different die.

 ## EVIDENCE

We know about the things sold in Viking shops from the objects dug up by archaeologists. In York, they could only dig up a small area, since the site of Jorvik has been built over many times since the Viking Age. But in Denmark and Sweden, the old market towns of Hedeby and Birka had been abandoned. At both of these sites, archaeologists found pieces of glassware and silk. They also found many everyday things, such as pins, needles, and spoons.

DID THE VIKINGS HAVE FAMILIES LIKE OURS?

A Viking's family included parents and children and also cousins, aunts, and uncles. Grandparents, parents, and children often lived together in the same house. The Vikings thought that loyalty to the family was more

important than loyalty to a leader. If someone was murdered, his family would murder someone from the killer's family. The two families might then be at war with each other for many years.

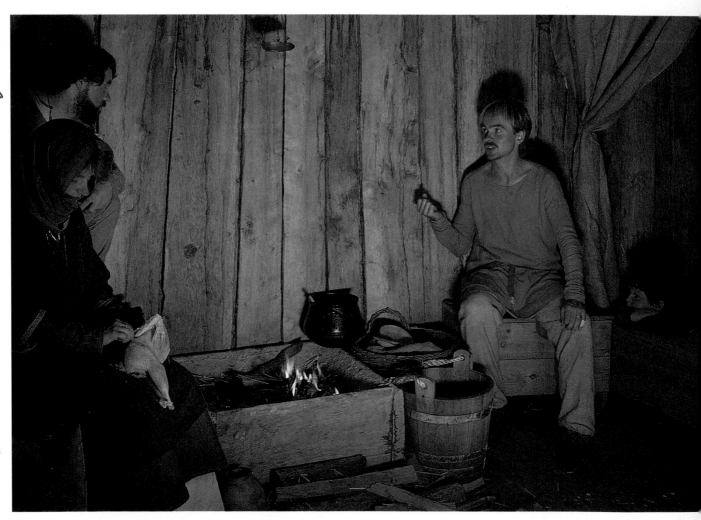

▲ THE FAMILY AT HOME

The fireplace was the most important place in the Viking home. The fire gave heat and light, and food was cooked over it. This picture of actors dressed as Vikings shows how the whole family would gather around the fireplace.

◀ VIKING WOMEN

This pendant on the left shows a Viking woman. Women were treated well. They could choose their own husband or stay single if they wanted to. If a woman's husband was away, the woman was left in charge of the house and business.

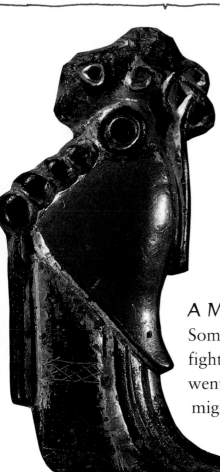

A MEMORIAL STONE ▶

Some Vikings were killed in fights or accidents when they went off raiding. Their families might put up a carved stone to remember them. This stone is from Sweden.

▼ USEFUL TOOLS

Viking clothes did not have pockets. Instead, Vikings carried the things they needed on a chain hanging from a brooch. These things included needles made out of fine bones. A woman also carried a knife, scissors, and keys to any chests in the house.

 MARRIAGE

Viking men and women could choose who they wanted to marry. They did not need permission from their parents. Most marriages took place in the early winter, when everyone was at home. The marriage was celebrated with a big feast shared by family, friends, and neighbors. The celebrations included eating and drinking and also poetry, music, and dancing. The occasion could last as long as two weeks. If the marriage did not work, it was very easy for the Viking couple to get a divorce.

Needles

Keys

Knife

Knife sheath

DID THE VIKINGS LIVE IN HOUSES?

Most Viking families lived on farms in the country. Their houses were known as longhouses, because of their shape. Often, Viking houses had only one large room or hall. Everyone ate and slept in this room. Sometimes, the barn for the animals was built on the end of the house. Only a small number of Vikings lived in towns.

◀ ▼ THE FARMHOUSE AT STONG

There are few Viking houses left today, because the houses were usually built out of wood, which rots. But a farmhouse at Stong in Iceland was dug up by **archaeologists** in 1939. There was enough of the building left to make the **reconstruction** below. The walls were made of blocks of turf, as shown on the left.

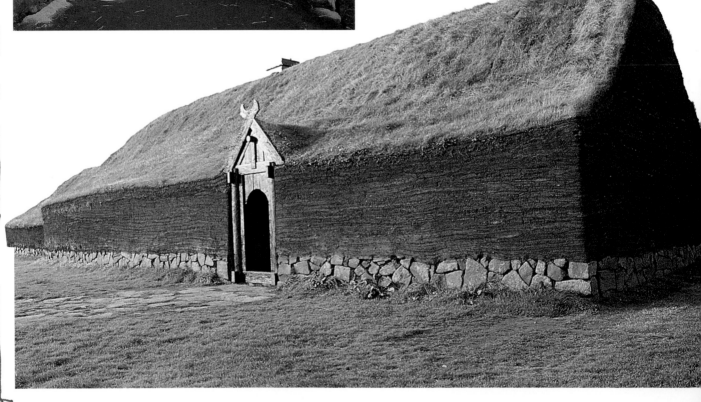

FURNITURE ▶

The Vikings did not have much furniture. Only the farmer and his wife slept in a bed. Everyone else slept on a raised ledge along the wall of the room. Spare clothes and blankets were kept in chests.

▼ KITCHEN UTENSILS

Vikings ate lots of dairy products made with the help of butter churns and cheese strainers. They stored food in wooden tubs. Flour often had pieces of stone in it. These came from the stones used to grind the grain. The stone wore the Vikings' teeth down!

Bed

Chest

▼ INSIDE A HOUSE

This reconstruction in Denmark shows the inside of a Viking house. The fireplace is in the middle of the room. A cooking pot is hanging from a chain from the roof. To the right of the door is the bed.

Wooden tub

Knife

Wooden bowls

Cheese drainer

 EATING MEALS

Vikings usually ate two meals a day. The first meal was eaten at eight o'clock in the morning and the second meal at seven o'clock at night. They used folding tables that were set up especially for meal times. Food was eaten from wooden bowls or plates. There were knives and spoons, but no forks.

WHO WENT TO WORK IN THE VIKING LANDS?

Most Vikings were freemen who owned their own land and worked for themselves. Their wives and children helped with the work. Some Vikings were slaves. They did heavy work like digging up **iron ore.** Some Vikings were traders as well as farmers, and some were craftsmen who made jewelry and weapons.

◀ MAKING A SWORD

This woodcarving shows a scene from the legend of Sigurd the Dragon-slayer. Sigurd and another Viking warrior named Reginn are making a sword. Sigurd works the bellows to keep the fire hot while Reginn hammers the blade of the sword flat.

Hammer

Shear

Tongs

▶ BLACKSMITH'S TOOLS

A Viking **blacksmith** used tools very much like those used today. His hammer had an iron head attached to a wooden handle. He smoothed rough edges of metal with a shear like the one on the right. He used iron tongs to bend hot metal into shape.

▼ ► MAKING BEADS

Craftsmen made beads from jet, amber, and crystal. They also made beads out of glass, like the ones shown here. The Vikings smelted the glass in small pots and pulled it into long sticks. The sticks were then wrapped around a metal rod. When the sticks hardened, the rod was taken out and the glass cut into beads. Glass sticks of different colors could be twisted together to make patterned beads.

Glass beads

▼ MAKING A COMB

The Vikings made their combs from pieces of deer antler (1). They cut a long strip of antler (2) and split it into two pieces along its length. This was for the top of the comb. They cut oblong pieces (3) which were slotted between the two long pieces and fixed together with nails. The oblong pieces were then sawed into teeth (4). A pattern was often made along the top of the comb.

SLAVES

There were three groups of slaves. The first group was made up of the children of slaves. The second group was prisoners taken in battle. The third group was people who had volunteered to become slaves so that they had food and somewhere to live. Slaves had no rights and no property. But a slave could work very hard and buy freedom for himself and his family.

WHAT DID THE VIKINGS DO ON THEIR VACATIONS?

The Vikings did not go away on vacation. But they did have three religious celebrations a year. These were Sigrblot in the summer, Vetrarblot after the harvest, and Jolablot after midwinter. At other times, the Vikings relaxed by ice skating, wrestling, swimming, and hunting.

▶ GAMES AND SKILLS

In bad weather, Vikings enjoyed playing board games. Some were played on boards like the one on the right. In good weather, they played a type of football. They also had rowing races and wrestling matches. Another test was to see who could walk all the way around a longship by balancing on its oars as the boat was being rowed.

◀ CHESS

The three chessmen on the left are from a set found on the Isle of Lewis in the Hebrides. They were carved in the twelfth century. Other Viking board games included hnefatafl. This had one playing piece like a king and the others pieces were plain. It is likely the king had to be defended from pieces on the other side.

ICE SKATING

When the rivers froze, the Vikings went ice skating. Skates were made from the foot bones of cattle and horses. They made a hole in the skate and stuck a peg in it. It was then tied to the shoe.

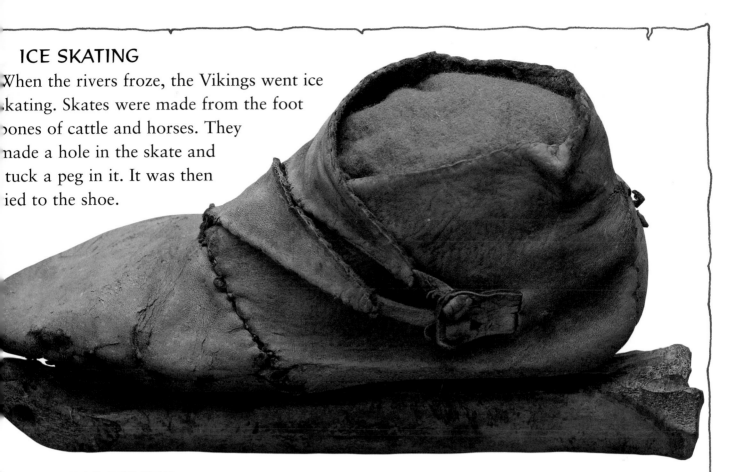

PLAYING PIECES

The Vikings used playing pieces made from wood, stone, ivory, and glass for their board games. These pieces are based on ones found in Birka.

Gambling pieces

DRINKING HORNS

Viking feasts could last for two weeks and involved a lot of drinking. The Vikings brewed beer and a drink called mead. They drank from horns like the one below.

Drinking horn

 SACRIFICES

At the three religious **feasts**, a horse was **sacrificed** to the gods. If the horse was killed, the meat from it was cooked and eaten by the Vikings. But sacrificed horses were not always killed. If the horse lived, the Viking shared the horse with the gods. It stayed with the Viking while it was useful to him. Then when the horse died, it belonged to the gods. We do not think that the Vikings sacrificed people.

WHAT DID THE VIKINGS WEAR?

Viking men wore tunics and tight-fitting pants. Women wore long dresses made of linen, which had a woolen tunic over the top. Everyone wore flat leather shoes, cloaks in cold weather, and jewelry. Pieces of Viking clothing have been dug up by **archaeologists**.

A VIKING FISHERMAN ▼

This model of a fisherman is in the Jorvik Museum. His head and face are the same size as those of a real Viking skull.

Shears

Ra
w

Wool comb

Loom

Reel

Spindle and whorl

▲ MAKING CLOTH

Viking women mostly made clothes from woolen cloth. Sheep's wool was cleaned and combed. It was then spun into yarn with a spindle and whorl. This yarn was wound on a reel and colored with vegetable dyes. It was then woven into cloth on a loom. Clay weights kept the threads hanging down in place.

SHOES ▶

To make a shoe, Vikings used a last like the one on the right. It was made of wood and shaped like a foot. The leather shoe was made around the last. Most shoes were held on the wearer's foot with a leather strip. Sometimes farmers made their own shoes, but there were also shoemakers in towns.

Last

Tortoise brooches

◀ BROOCHES

The Vikings fastened their clothes with belts or brooches. The brooches shown above were called tortoise brooches because of their shape. They had a pin underneath, and Viking women threaded this pin through a long loop at the back of their tunics. It then went through a shorter loop at the front. A string of beads showed how wealthy a family was. Both men and women used large pins to fasten their cloaks in the winter.

HYGIENE

It is hard to know whether the Vikings were clean or dirty. Men in England complained about their women liking the Vikings who combed their hair, bathed, and changed their clothes so often! But an Arab who wrote about the Vikings said they did not wash often enough. Because lots of combs have been found, it seems that the Vikings took care of their hair. Men fastened their hair back with a band. They kept their beards and moustaches neatly trimmed. Married women covered their hair with a scarf.

WHO DID THE VIKINGS WORSHIP?

The early Vikings had many different gods and goddesses. They thought the gods lived in a place called Asgard. The Vikings themselves lived in Midgard and beyond this was Utgard, where the Frost Giants lived. They believed that one day the Frost Giants would destroy all the gods, bringing the world to an end.

Loki

ODIN AND LOKI ▲▼

Odin was the most important Viking god. He was the wise god of poets and the god of kings and warriors. Legends said that Loki, the mischief-maker, once had his lips sewn together as a punishment.

Odin

◀ STAVE CHURCHES

There are still some ancient churches in Scandinavia. This one is at Borgund in Norway. They are called stave churches, because their walls are made of upright planks of wood, called staves. By the time they were built, the Viking Age was over. The people of the Viking lands had become Christians.

Thor's hammer

▼ MAKING THOR'S HAMMER

The craftsman made a model of the hammer in wax (1). He pressed the model in clay to make a mold (2). The mold was heated to melt the wax. It ran out of a hole and left the shape of the hammer behind (3). Melted silver was poured into the mold. When it was hard, the silver hammer was taken out (4).

1.

2.

3.

4.

▲ THOR AND HIS HAMMER

Thor was the most popular Viking god. He was thought to be a huge man with a red beard. He made thunder rumble by riding across the sky in a chariot pulled by goats. Thor was not as clever as Odin. He had to use a hammer as a weapon in his battles with the giants. Many Vikings wore a small copy of his hammer. They thought it would protect them from bad luck.

HOW THE VIKINGS BECAME CHRISTIANS

The Vikings who traveled were the first to become Christians. This was because it was easier to trade with Christian merchants if they shared the same religion. But Christianity did not spread widely until the late Viking Age. The Vikings in

Iceland voted on religion in 1000 CE. Half of them voted to become Christians. The other half voted to keep worshiping the old gods. Christianity finally won, but people could still worship the old gods in secret.

DID THE VIKINGS BELIEVE IN LIFE AFTER DEATH?

Viking warriors thought that if they died in battle, they would go to a place called Valhalla. There, they would be able to kill each other all day long. In the evening, they would go back to Odin's hall and come back to life again. After feasting, they would be ready to fight again the next morning. But if Vikings died in bed, they would go to a cold, frosty place.

◄ GRAVE GOODS

Men and women were given **grave goods** for their journey to the next life. This Viking warrior's grave was dug up in Norway. Only part of the warrior's skeleton was left. His sword was by his right hand and pieces of his shield were on his chest. A dead warrior was given food and beverages for the journey to Valhalla. Traders were often buried with some of the goods they traded.

Grave goods

THE JOURNEY TO VALHALLA ▶

On the right is a picture stone from Sweden. It shows how warriors who die in battle go to Valhalla. The bottom picture shows them traveling there in a longship. The top picture shows a warrior arriving at Valhalla. He has been brought back to life and given a horse. He is being offered a drink before going to the feast in Odin's hall.

STONE SHIPS

Important Vikings were buried in their ships, but most Vikings were buried in ordinary graves. These were often marked with stones in the shape of a ship. The photograph above shows a grave in Denmark.

CREMATION

Not all Vikings were buried. Some were burned or **cremated**. A Viking **chieftain** was cremated at the river Volga in 922. First, wood was piled up on the riverbank. Then the chieftain's ship was lifted on top of the wood and his body was carried on board the ship.

Food for the dead man included two cows and a cockerel. A slave girl was then **sacrificed** on board. The chieftain's men watched as the wood was set alight. When everything in the ship had burned, the ashes were placed in a special grave. This was called a memorial mound.

WHO RULED THE VIKINGS?

The early Vikings had no rulers. The local government, called a **Thing**, set the laws. Freemen had the right to vote in the Thing. The most powerful man in an area became the leader, or jarl. Jarls, also known as kings, only ruled a small area. Later, kings ruled Denmark, Norway, and Sweden.

THINGVELLIR ▼

Iceland did not have a king during the Viking Age. Instead, the people were ruled by two Things. The lower Thing looked after local issues. The higher level was the Althing. This met at Thingvellir, which is shown in the photograph. The Althing met for two weeks at midsummer every year. Only the men could vote, but they took their families to Thingvellir with them.

OUTLAWS

Most Vikings obeyed the laws of the Things. Anyone who did not, became an outlaw. An outlaw had to give up all his land and leave the country as quickly as possible. This was because anyone could kill an outlaw without being punished. Eric the Red was outlawed from Norway in 980. He went to Iceland, but was soon outlawed there, too.

▲ THE KING OF NORWAY

The picture above is from a book called the Flateyjarbok. It shows Harold Finehair, the first king to rule over Norway.

Coins of Viking kings

▶ JEWELING STONE

The stone on the right was set up in Jelling in Denmark. It has three sides. The one you can see here shows an imaginary animal with a snake wrapped around its body. The stone was put up by King Harold (also called Harold Bluetooth) in the tenth century. It was in memory of his parents.

WERE THERE ANY VIKING ARTISTS?

No pictures have been found from the Viking Age. But many Vikings carved designs into stone and wood. Many of the patterns are done in the "gripping beast" design. When you look at the swirling patterns, you can see animals gripping each other.

▶ THE OSBERG CARVINGS

Archaeologists found many woodcarvings on the Oseberg ship. There were four posts with animal heads, like the one on the right. The posts are all different. But each animal has a fierce look on its face. This was probably supposed to scare off evil spirits. Carved sleds, a wagon, and a bed were also found on the ship. Because wood rots, only a small amount of carving from Viking times has survived. It seems that farmers spent their spare time carving patterns when the weather was too bad to work.

Gripping beast brooch

◀ GOLD COINS

The iron axe on the extreme left was probably made for use on special occasions. A pattern has been cut into it and decorated with silver wire. Next to it is a silver brooch from Sweden. It was made around 940. The beast's paws grip the sides of the brooch in this simple gripping beast design.

WOOD CARVING

These carved panels are on the wall of the church at Urnes in Norway. They were carved in the eleventh century. They stand for Yggdrasil, or the World Tree. The Vikings thought Yggdrasil held the universe together. Its branches reached the sky and covered the Earth.

◀ JEWELRY

The brooch on the left was probably used to fasten a woman's shawl. Rich people had jewelry made of gold or silver. Poorer people wore brooches made from cheaper metals. These brooches were sometimes covered in a layer of gilt or tin to make them look like gold or silver.

▶ STONE CARVING

The Vikings rarely carved pictures of people. This means that the cross in the drawing on the right is unusual. It was found in Yorkshire and shows a warrior from the tenth century. He is wearing a cone-shaped helmet. He has a sword, an axe, a knife, and a spear.

The Middleton Cross

DID THE VIKINGS WRITE BOOKS?

The Vikings were great storytellers and poets, but they didn't write books. One reason was that they did not have an alphabet like ours. They used **runes** instead. But the Vikings told stories and poems that were passed down from one generation to another. Many stories survived and were written down after the Viking Age.

PICTURE STONES ▶

The Vikings enjoyed telling stories about the gods. Sometimes they carved these stories on memorial stones. The stone on the right is from a story about Odin. The Vikings liked stories about Thor best. He got into fights with the Frost Giants (see page 26). Once he stole a jug of beer from the Frost Giants, so that the gods could have a party!

RUNES ▶

The Vikings only had 16 letters in their alphabet. These letters were called runes. The early Vikings thought the runes were magic. They scratched them on a sword to make it stronger. Later, the Vikings used runes for writing on memorial stones.

POETRY ▶

The Vikings loved poetry. When they had a feast, a poet was usually invited to tell poems after the meal. He would make up new poems or recite old ones. Some poets traveled around the country making up verses praising their hosts. If the host liked the verses, he gave the poet a generous gift, such as this silver armlet. The most famous Viking poet was Egil Skallagrimsson. He once saved his life with a poem praising his enemy.

GOOD ADVICE

The Havamal was a Viking book. It was supposed to have Odin's advice to the Vikings in it. He told them:

"Look carefully around doorways before you go in— you never know when an enemy might be there."

"There is no better load a man can carry than much common sense—no worse a load than too much drink."

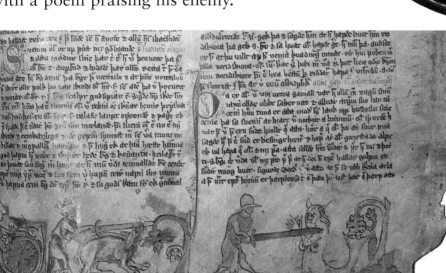

▲ THE SAGAS

The Viking Sagas were legends written down in the thirteenth century. Many of them were adventures of Vikings who had moved from Norway to Iceland. Some of the books have little pictures in them. The pictures above show Olaf Tryggvason killing a wild boar and a sea ogress.

HOW DID THE VIKINGS TRAVEL?

The Viking homelands were covered with marshes, lakes, and mountains. This made it impossible to travel easily by land. Most Vikings lived near the sea and traveled by ship or boat. Their ships were made to sail on the open sea and in shallow water, too. This meant they could travel a long way inland on rivers.

▶ BUILDING A LONGSHIP

The trunk of an oak tree was used for the **keel** of the ship. Curved stems were nailed to each end of the keel. Wedge-shaped planks were then nailed to the keel. Each plank fitted over the next. Cross-beams were added to the inside. Then the **keelson** was fitted to hold up the mast and its sail.

Oak keel

Cross beams

Curved stems

Keelson supporting mast

▲ THE OSEBERG SHIP

This ship was used for the burial at Oseberg in Norway. Earth had been piled over it. This had kept the air out and stopped the wood from rotting. It was buried in around 850. **Archaeologists** were able to repair it so that it now looks very much as it did in Viking times.

THE OSEBERG WAGON ▶

This wooden wagon was found on the Oseberg ship. It belonged to a royal lady. It is covered in carvings. They tell the legend of Sigurd the Dragon-slayer. Most Viking wagons were made like this one, so that the body could be lifted off the wheels. Wagons used every day were much plainer.

▶ SHIP CARVINGS

This carved stone from Gotland shows a ship in full sail. The Vikings also rowed their ships.

Viking coins

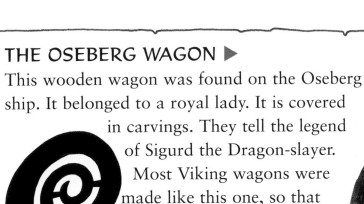

◀ SHIPS ON COINS

We can work out how the sails and rigging worked on Viking ships by looking at pictures on coins.

 ## NAVIGATION

The Vikings liked to sail close to land if possible. On the open sea, they had to find their way by watching the Sun and the stars. They had weathervanes on their ships. These had long streamers that blew in the direction of the wind.

HOW FAR DID THE VIKINGS SAIL?

The Vikings were great adventurers. At first, their journeys took them to the Faeroes, Shetlands, and Orkneys. They then reached the coasts of Scotland, England, Wales, and Ireland. Vikings from Norway settled in Iceland in 874. From there, they sailed on to reach Greenland around 980.

TRADE ▶

The **grave goods** buried with tradesmen tell **archaeologists** how far the Vikings traveled. These pots may have been brought back to Sweden from Eastern Europe.

▼ TRADE

We can also see how far the Vikings traveled by the things that have been dug up in places where they settled. Enough pieces of wood were found in Newfoundland to make the reconstruction of this longboat.

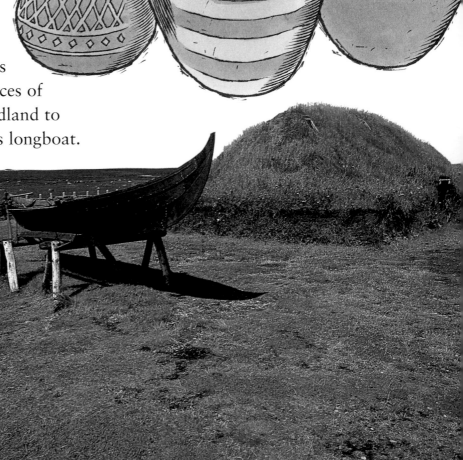

▶ GREENLAND

This picture shows what is left of a Viking settlement in Greenland. Eric the Red took people there around 985. The settlers from Iceland took animals with them on their ships. Because of the bad weather in Greenland, the Vikings eventually left their farms there.

▶ TRADE ROUTES

By sailing along rivers, the Vikings could reach Arabia. They could get luxury goods there such as silk and spices.

Timber	Amber	Copper	Spices
	Fish	Tin	Wool
Iron	Corn	Lead	Wine
Furs	Salt	Slaves	
Honey		Silks	
Wax	Silver		

ICELAND

Bergen

Novgorod

Kiev

Black Sea

NORTH AFRICA

Mediterranean Sea

▼ SILVER TREASURE

The silver Viking objects below were all found together in Lancashire, England. Many were **Anglo-Saxon**. Others came from Arabia and the continent of Europe.

◉ TRAVEL PROBLEMS ◉

At sea, the ships of Viking traders might be wrecked in a storm. And on rivers, there were **rapids** to get past. The Vikings did this by lifting their ships out of the water and putting them on wooden rollers. The ships could then be pushed overland and tipped back into the water on the other side of the rapids.

DID THE VIKINGS HAVE AN ARMY?

The first Viking armies were small groups of warriors. They fought for themselves and not for their country. Later, Vikings started to fight for their king. These armies were more organized. In 1016, the King of Denmark's army defeated the English at Ashingdon. This meant that England had a Danish king.

▶ ▼ VIKING WARRIORS

Viking warriors protected their bodies with a shield and wore a helmet. Usually, helmets were made of leather, but some helmets were made of iron, like this one on the right. Helmets never had horns on them. The Lewis chessman below looks ready to fight on horseback. The Vikings usually rode to the battlefield, where they then fought on foot.

Sword

Battle axe

Shield

Spear

Scabbard

▲ WEAPONS

A Viking's favorite weapon was his sword. It was used to slash at the enemy rather than stab him. Vikings also used spears and battle-axes. Shields were made of wood and covered with leather.

🗡 BATTLE TACTICS 🗡

Viking armies were never big, so they had to take their enemy by surprise. If the enemy were winning, the Vikings fought from behind a wall of shields.

DANISH BARRACKS ▶

The picture on the right is a model of a Viking site found in Denmark. The site may have been soldiers' **barracks**.

WHAT HAPPENED TO THE VIKINGS?

The Viking Age was over by 1100. In places such as Britain and Normandy, the Vikings had made homes and married local women. In Scandinavia, more land was being farmed. This meant that young men no longer went abroad to find farms of their own.

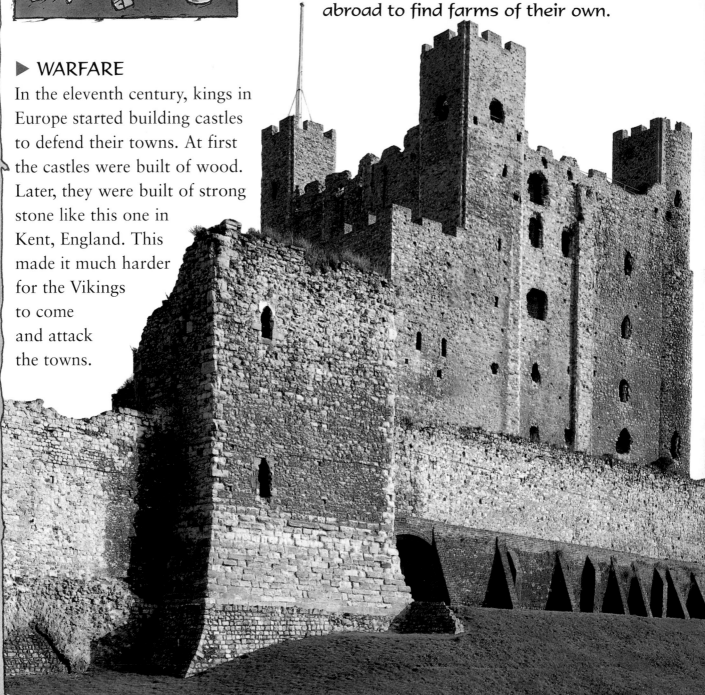

▶ WARFARE

In the eleventh century, kings in Europe started building castles to defend their towns. At first the castles were built of wood. Later, they were built of strong stone like this one in Kent, England. This made it much harder for the Vikings to come and attack the towns.

▼ AFTER THE VIKINGS

Stone carvers in England used Viking designs after 1100. These pillars are by the door of a church in Hertfordshire. They were carved in the late twelfth century. The carver used Viking gripping beasts and serpents in his design.

Church door carvings

▼ THE NORMANS

The Bayeux Tapestry is a long strip of embroidery. It tells the story of the Norman Conquest of England. In 1066, William, Duke of Normandy, became King of England. He was related to the famous Viking, Rollo. But the Normans did not live like Vikings. They spoke French and were Christians. Their soldiers wore coats of chain mail, which you can see in the scene below.

THE VIKING HERITAGE

Many English words that we use today were first used by the Vikings. These include sky, bread, egg, scrawny, snort, and lump. Many place names in Britain also come from the Viking Age. Names ending in "wick" were markets. Names ending in "by" were villages. And names ending in "haven" were harbors. Another Viking word used in place names is "ness." This means a headland.

GLOSSARY, FURTHER INFORMATION, AND WEB SITES

ANGLES People from northern Germany who settled in eastern and northern England in the fifth century CE.

ANGLO-SAXON A member of one of the Germanic peoples, the Angles, the Saxons, and the Jutes, who settled in Britain in the fifth and sixth centuries.

ARCHAEOLOGIST A scientist who makes a study of the remains of the past.

BARRACKS A building where soldiers live together.

BLACKSMITH A craftsman who forges and shapes iron with an anvil and hammer.

CE The abbreviation of "Christian era," used to show that a date is of the present era, which started with the birth of Christ.

CHIEFTAIN The leader of a tribe.

CREMATE When someone's body is burned rather than being buried.

DANGELD Money paid to the Vikings so they would go away and not attack.

DIE A tool used for shaping metal.

FRISIANS People from the Frisian Islands or Friesland.

GRAVE GOODS Special objects buried with a body. Viking grave goods included food and often the Viking's sword.

HARROW A frame of wood or iron with spikes, used to push the soil over freshly sown seeds.

IRON ORE Rocks from which the metal iron can be taken out.

JUTES People from northwest Germany, who settled in southeast England in the fifth century CE.

KEEL The part of a ship that goes from end to end and supports the ship.

KEELSON The part of a ship that supports the mast.

MONASTERIES Places where religious men called monks live and work.

RAPIDS A part of a river where the current is very fast and strong.

RECONSTRUCTION An object which has been made to look like the original.

RUNES Sticklike letters of the alphabet, used by Scandinavians and Anglo-Saxons, that could be carved on stone, metal, or wood.

SACRIFICE A valuable offering made to please a god.

THING The local meeting that decided Viking rules.

TRADING CENTERS Towns where tradesmen and craftsmen sold their goods.

Books to read

Life of the Ancient Vikings
by Hazel Richardson (Crabtree Publishing, 2005)

People of the Ancient World: The Vikings
by Virginia Schomp (Children's Press, 2005)

Vikings: Raiders and Explorers
by Aileen Weintraub (Children's Press, 2003)

Web Sites

Due to the changing nature of Internet links, PowerKids Press has developed an online list of Web sites related to the subject of this book. This site is updated regularly. Please use this link to access this list:
www.powerkidslinks.com/flash/vikings

INDEX